FROM METRICS TO INSIGHTS

How To Measure The Impact Of Your Marketing Efforts"

Pius Borr

1

Table of Contents

CHAPTER 15

CONCLUSION: The Future of Marketing Measurement and Analytics

INTRODUCTION

Welcome to the world of marketing! In today's ever-evolving digital landscape, businesses must be agile and adaptable to stay competitive. As such, measuring the impact of your marketing efforts is critical to ensuring that your strategy is effective and aligned with your business goals.

Though it can be intimidating, assessing marketing activities is crucial for success. Data must be gathered and analyzed to learn how well your efforts are working.

The ability to evaluate and translate metrics into useful insights that might spur corporate growth is just as important as simply tracking them.

The process of going from numbers to insights will be covered in this article, along with best practices for evaluating the success of your marketing initiatives.

This manual will give you the tools and expertise required to accurately gauge your marketing performance and promote business success, regardless of your level of experience in the industry.

Let's get started and learn how you can use data to acquire insights that will help you improve your marketing plan and accomplish your business goals.

One of the most important steps in the marketing process is measuring the results of your marketing activities. It enables you to assess the success of your efforts and pinpoint potential improvement areas.

Nonetheless, the method for assessing marketing performance has drastically changed over time. It can be difficult to decide which metrics are the most crucial given the proliferation of digital marketing and the number of variables that marketers can now track.

The idea of switching from metrics to insights is applicable in this situation. The objective is to comprehend the meaning of the data and how it can be used to fuel corporate growth, not just to gather it.

In order and understand consumer behavior, preferences, and needs, data must be interpreted. By doing this, you can find ways to improve your marketing campaigns, boost customer engagement, and raise sales.

We'll look at the many metrics you should be monitoring in this tutorial, such as website traffic, social media engagement, and conversion rates. We'll also go over how crucial it is to establish precise corporate objectives and match your marketing initiatives to these objectives. We will also look at several tools and methods for data analysis and producing useful insights.

CHAPTER 1

UNDERSTANDING THE IMPORTANCE OF MEASURING MARKETING IMPACT

Marketing is a critical component of any business, and it is essential to measure the impact of marketing efforts to ensure that they are achieving the desired outcomes.

In today's rapidly evolving digital landscape, marketers have access to a wealth of data that can be used to measure the impact of their campaigns. However, tracking metrics is not enough; marketers must be able to analyze and interpret data to derive insights that can drive business growth.

In this chapter, we will explore the importance of measuring marketing impact and the challenges that marketers face in doing so.

We will also discuss the role of data in marketing, including the types of data that can be collected and the tools and techniques for analyzing data.

The Importance of Measuring Marketing Impact

Measuring marketing impact is critical to achieving business objectives. By tracking key performance indicators (KPIs) such as website traffic, social media engagement, and conversion rates, marketers can evaluate the effectiveness of their campaigns and identify areas for improvement.

This allows businesses to optimize their marketing strategy and allocate resources more effectively.

Measuring marketing impact is also essential for demonstrating the value of marketing efforts to stakeholders. By providing clear metrics and insights, marketers can communicate the impact of their campaigns and justify their budget to senior executives.

Challenges in Measuring Marketing Impact

Despite the importance of measuring marketing impact, marketers face several challenges in doing so. One of the biggest challenges is identifying the right metrics to track. With so many metrics available, it can be challenging to determine which ones are the most important for achieving business objectives.

Another challenge is collecting and analyzing data. With the vast amounts of data available, it can be overwhelming to manage and analyze data effectively.

Additionally, data can be scattered across multiple platforms and systems, making it difficult to consolidate and analyze.

The Role of Data in Marketing

Data plays a critical role in marketing, providing insights into customer behavior, preferences, and needs. By collecting and analyzing data, marketers can gain a better understanding of their target audience and tailor their marketing strategy accordingly. There are several types of data that marketers can collect, including demographic data, behavioral data, and transactional data.

To analyze data effectively, marketers must use appropriate tools and techniques. This includes data analytics software, data visualization tools, and statistical analysis methods. By using these tools, marketers can turn data into actionable insights that can drive business growth.

Marketers also face the challenge of measuring the impact of offline marketing efforts, such as events or print advertising. While it is possible to track metrics such as attendance or the number of leads generated from an event, it can be difficult to tie these metrics to specific business outcomes. However, with the help of technology and data analytics, it is becoming increasingly possible to track the impact of offline marketing efforts.

Another challenge in measuring marketing impact is the ever-changing nature of the digital landscape. As new technologies and platforms emerge, marketers must adapt their measurement strategies to stay relevant.

For example, the rise of mobile devices has led to a shift in website traffic patterns, with an increasing number of users accessing websites on mobile devices. As a result, marketers must ensure that their measurement strategies account for mobile traffic and engagement.

Despite these challenges, there are numerous benefits to measuring marketing impact. In addition to optimizing marketing efforts and justifying marketing budgets, measuring marketing impact can also help businesses identify new opportunities and areas for growth.

By analyzing data and identifying trends, marketers can develop new products or services, target new customer segments, or expand into new markets.

Measuring marketing impact is critical to achieving business objectives and demonstrating the value of marketing efforts to stakeholders. However, marketers face several challenges in doing so, including identifying the right metrics and managing and analyzing data effectively.

By understanding the importance of measuring marketing impact and using appropriate tools and techniques, marketers can turn data into insights that can optimize their marketing strategy and drive business success.

CHAPTER 2

SETTING BUSINESS OBJECTIVES AND ALIGNING METRICS

In Chapter 1, we discussed the importance of measuring marketing impact and the challenges that marketers face in doing so. In this chapter, we will explore how to set business objectives and align metrics to ensure that marketing efforts are focused on achieving specific goals.

Setting Business Objectives

Before any marketing campaign is launched, it is important to set clear business objectives. Business objectives should be specific, measurable, achievable, relevant, and time-bound (SMART). This ensures that marketing efforts are aligned with business goals and can be measured effectively.

Business objectives can vary depending on the organization and the marketing campaign. For example, a business objective may be to increase website traffic, generate more leads, or improve customer engagement.

It is important to ensure that business objectives are aligned with the overall business strategy and that they are realistic and achievable.

Aligning Metrics

Once business objectives have been set, it is important to identify the metrics that will be used to measure progress toward those objectives. Metrics should be aligned with the business objectives and should be specific, measurable, relevant, and timely.

For example, if the business objective is to increase website traffic, the relevant metrics may include page views, unique visitors, and bounce rate. If the business objective is to generate more leads, the relevant metrics may include conversion rate, form submissions, and lead quality.

It is important to select the right metrics to ensure that marketing efforts are focused on achieving specific goals. Selecting the wrong metrics can result in wasted resources and ineffective marketing campaigns.

Data Collection and Analysis

To measure marketing impact effectively, it is important to collect and analyze data. This includes both quantitative data, such as website traffic and conversion rates, and qualitative data, such as customer feedback and sentiment analysis.

Using software like Google Analytics or social media analytics platforms, data collecting can be automated. Moreover, questionnaires and forms for consumer feedback can be used to collect data. After data has been gathered, it is crucial to analyze it to gain knowledge that will help with marketing strategy.

Data analysis can be done manually or through the use of data analytics software. Data visualization tools such as dashboards and charts can be used to present data in a meaningful way that can inform decision-making.

Together with establishing precise company goals and coordinating measurements, it's crucial to make sure that all stakeholders are on the same page.

It's crucial to regularly assess the impact of marketing and change as necessary. The performance of marketing efforts can be improved through adjustments and alterations. Marketers can find areas for improvement and implement changes to increase campaign effectiveness by routinely gauging the impact of their marketing efforts and evaluating data.

Ultimately, it is crucial to measure marketing impact in the context of the broader business plan. Even if marketing is only one component of the jigsaw, it is crucial to make sure that all marketing initiatives are in line with the overarching business plan.

This entails taking into account elements including the level of competition, market trends, and client preferences and wants.

In general, establishing company goals and coordinating KPIs are necessary for accurately assessing the impact of marketing. Marketing professionals may improve their campaigns and help businesses succeed by choosing the appropriate metrics to track progress toward particular objectives and by evaluating data to conclude.

The success of digital marketing strategies, such as search engine optimization (SEO), social media, and email marketing, will be examined in the following chapter.

CHAPTER 3

MEASURING THE EFFECTIVENESS of Digital MARKETING CAMPAIGNS

Digital marketing has become an essential part of modern marketing strategy. In this chapter, we will explore how to measure the effectiveness of digital marketing campaigns, including search engine optimization (SEO), social media, and email marketing.

Search Engine Optimization (SEO)

Search engine optimization (SEO) is the process of optimizing a website to improve its ranking in search engine results pages (SERPs). SEO can be a powerful tool for driving website traffic and generating leads, but it requires careful monitoring and measurement to be effective.

Several metrics can be used to measure the effectiveness of SEO, including:

- **Organic search traffic:** The number of visitors to a website that comes from organic search results.

- **Keyword rankings:** The position of a website in search engine results for specific keywords.

- **Click-through rate (CTR):** The percentage of users who click on a website in search engine results.

- **Bounce rate:** The percentage of users who leave a website after viewing only one page.

- **Conversion rate:** The percentage of website visitors who take a desired action, such as filling out a form or making a purchase.

- **Engagement rate:** The percentage of social media followers who engage with a post, such as by liking, commenting, or sharing.

- **Reach** The number of unique users who see a social media post.

By tracking these metrics over time, marketers can identify trends and make adjustments to their SEO strategy to improve performance.

Social Media

Social media has grown to be a crucial component of contemporary marketing strategy since it allows businesses to communicate with a broad audience using focused messaging. Yet, given the variety of measures to take into account, determining the efficacy of social media can be difficult.

To measure the effectiveness of social media marketing, it is important to track these metrics over time and identify trends. By experimenting with different types of content and messaging, marketers can optimize their social media strategy to drive engagement and conversions.

Email Marketing

Email marketing remains one of the most effective digital marketing channels for generating leads and driving conversions. However, measuring the effectiveness of email marketing requires careful attention to metrics.

It is important to monitor these data over time and experiment with various forms of messaging and calls to action to gauge the efficacy of email marketing. Marketers may increase engagement and conversions by optimizing email messages based on performance data.

In conclusion, measuring the effectiveness of digital marketing campaigns requires careful attention to metrics and a willingness to experiment and adjust strategy based on performance data. By tracking metrics such as organic search traffic, engagement rate, and open rate, marketers can identify trends and optimize their campaigns for success.

In the next chapter, we will explore how to use marketing analytics to gain deeper insights into marketing performance and drive business success.

CHAPTER 4

GAINING MORE INSIGHTS FROM MARKETING ANALYTICS

To gain insights and promote corporate performance, marketing analytics refers to the procedure of gathering, evaluating, and analyzing marketing data.

This chapter will examine the use of marketing analytics to enhance campaign effectiveness and obtain deeper insights into marketing performance.

Gathering Marketing Information

The correct data must be gathered to apply marketing analytics effectively. Data on website traffic, social media activity, email open rates, and other statistics may be included. Google Analytics, social media analytics programs, and email marketing platforms are just a few of the technologies available for gathering marketing data.

Marketing Performance Evaluation

After gathering marketing data, it's crucial to evaluate performance using key metrics. Depending on the particular marketing campaign, these metrics may differ, but they may include things like website traffic, engagement rate, conversion rate, and return on investment (ROI).

Data Analysis for Marketing

Understanding what is and is not working in a marketing effort can be gained from analyzing marketing data. This might entail spotting trends, assessing performance versus standards, and pinpointing areas that require improvement.

Using data visualization tools, such as charts and graphs, is one efficient way to analyze marketing data. While analyzing raw data, these methods can be used to spot patterns and trends in the data that may not be immediately obvious.

Optimizing Marketing Campaigns

Marketers can decide how to best optimize their marketing campaigns based on the insights gleaned through marketing analytics. Making adjustments to the targeting, messaging, or channels utilized to communicate with the target audience may be necessary.

Marketing analytics includes a critical component called continuous optimization. By routinely gathering and evaluating data, marketers can identify areas for improvement and make changes to increase performance.

Marketing analytics is a crucial instrument for developing a deeper understanding of marketing performance and successful campaign optimization. Marketers may propel corporate success and meet their marketing objectives by gathering the appropriate data, evaluating performance against key indicators, analyzing data to find patterns and areas for improvement, and refining campaigns based on insights obtained through marketing analytics.

As new technologies develop, marketers must stay current with the newest tools and approaches for gathering and analyzing data because the field of marketing analytics is continuously changing.

The application of artificial intelligence and machine learning is one trend in marketing analytics that is quickly gaining prominence.

When analyzing marketing data, patterns and trends that may not be immediately obvious when looking at raw data can be found with the use of AI and machine learning algorithms.

For instance, based on previous data and additional considerations like the time of day and audience demographics, an AI algorithm may be able to determine which social media posts are most likely to produce engagement.

The requirement to blend quantitative data with qualitative insights is another critical component of marketing analytics. Insights into performance can be gained through quantitative statistics, but it's also crucial to get qualitative feedback from clients and other stakeholders to fully comprehend their wants and needs.

Ultimately, marketers must employ marketing analytics to spur action and inform choices. The ultimate objective of data collection and analysis is to get insights from marketing analytics that can be used to improve campaigns and spur corporate success.

CHAPTER 5

THE ROLE OF ATTRIBUTION MODELING IN MEASURING MARKETING IMPACT

Attribution modeling is a process that allows marketers to measure the impact of different marketing channels and campaigns on customer behavior and sales. In this chapter, we will explore the role of attribution modeling in measuring marketing impact and how to choose the right attribution model for your business.

Understanding Attribution Modeling

Attribution modeling is the process of assigning credit to different marketing channels and touchpoints for driving a specific action, such as a purchase or a lead.

This is important because most customer journeys involve multiple touch points across different marketing channels, and it can be difficult to determine which touchpoints are most influential in driving conversions.

Attribution modeling can also help marketers identify which marketing channels and touchpoints are most effective at driving conversions, which can inform budget allocation and optimization strategies.

For example, if a certain channel or touchpoint consistently drives high-converting traffic, marketers can allocate more budget to that channel or optimize their campaigns to target that touchpoint more effectively.

However, attribution modeling is not a perfect science, and there are several challenges that marketers may face when implementing attribution modeling.

One of the biggest challenges is accurately tracking and measuring the impact of offline channels, such as print ads or events, which can be difficult to track using digital analytics tools.

There are several different attribution models that marketers can use to assign credit to different touchpoints, including:

First-touch attribution: This model assigns all credit for a conversion to the first touchpoint a customer interacts with.

Last-touch attribution: This model assigns all credit for a conversion to the last touchpoint a customer interacts with.

Linear attribution: This model assigns equal credit to all touchpoints in the customer journey.

Time decay attribution: This model assigns more credit to touchpoints that occur closer to the conversion.

Choosing the Right Attribution Model

Choosing the right attribution model depends on several factors, including the complexity of your customer journey, the length of your sales cycle, and the types of marketing channels and touchpoints you use.

For example, if your sales cycle is short and most conversions happen after only one or two touchpoints, a first-touch or last-touch attribution model may be appropriate.

However, if your sales cycle is longer and involves multiple touchpoints across different channels, a linear or time decay attribution model may be more accurate.

It is also important to consider the limitations of each attribution model. For example, first-touch attribution may not give enough credit to touchpoints that occur later in the customer journey, while last-touch attribution may not give enough credit to touchpoints that introduce customers to your brand.

Implementing Attribution Modeling

Implementing attribution modeling requires collecting and analyzing data from multiple marketing channels and touchpoints.

This may involve using tools such as Google Analytics, marketing automation platforms, and customer relationship management (CRM) systems to track customer behavior and conversions across different channels.

It is also important to regularly review and update your attribution model based on changes in your marketing strategy and customer behavior. For example, if you start using a new marketing channel that drives significant conversions, you may need to update your attribution model to give that channel more credit.

Another challenge is the lack of standardization in attribution modeling, which can make it difficult to compare results across different campaigns or businesses.

To address this challenge, marketers can use industry-standard attribution models, such as the Markov chain model or the Shapley value model, or work with analytics experts to develop a customized attribution model that best fits their business needs.

Attribution modeling is a potent tool for assessing the influence of various marketing touchpoints and channels on consumer behavior and sales.

Marketers may obtain important insights into the efficiency of their marketing initiatives and optimize them for success by selecting the appropriate attribution model, putting data gathering and analysis tools in place, and routinely assessing and upgrading their attribution model.

To create a tailored strategy that best meets your company's goals, you should consult with analytics professionals and be aware of the difficulties and restrictions associated with attribution modeling.

CHAPTER 6

ASSESSING BRAND EQUITY AND AWARENESS

Brand equity and awareness are crucial factors for determining whether your marketing efforts were successful.

This chapter will cover the value of evaluating brand equity and awareness, as well as the many metrics and methods available for doing so and how to utilize the results to guide your marketing plan.

Why Assess Brand Equity and Awareness?

Brand equity is the value that your brand provides to your goods or services, whereas brand awareness measures how familiar people are with your brand. These indicators need to be measured for several reasons.

- They can assist you in monitoring the success of your efforts to create your brand over time.

- Exposing areas that could require more attention or resources, might help your marketing approach.

- They can aid in locating opportunities to set your brand apart from rivals.

Brand Awareness Metrics

To assess brand awareness, you can use several measures and methods, such as:

Reach The total population to which your brand or marketing communications are presented.

Impressions: The number of times people are exposed to your brand or marketing communications.

Share of voice: The proportion of discussions or references to your brand that occur in your market or industry.

Surveys: You can use surveys or focus groups to find out how people feel about your brand.

Assessment of Brand Equity

Compared to measuring brand awareness, measuring brand equity entails determining how people view the value of your brand. You may gauge brand equity using a variety of indicators and instruments, such as:

- The Net Promoter Score (NPS) metric analyzes how likely it is for customers to tell others about your brand.

- The proportion of customers that consistently use your goods or services is known as brand loyalty.

Brand associations: Qualities or traits that customers relate to your brand by Measurements for Brand Awareness and Equity Used to Guide Marketing Strategy

You can use this data to guide your marketing approach after measuring your brand equity and awareness. For instance:

If there is little knowledge of your business, you might want to concentrate on expanding reach and impressions through content marketing or advertising.

If your brand's equity is low, you might want to concentrate on creating brand associations that set it apart from rivals, including highlighting its sustainability or customer service.

If your brand equity is strong, you might want to concentrate on using it to break into new markets or product categories.

To sum up, evaluating brand equity and awareness is crucial for gauging the efficacy of your marketing initiatives and guiding your marketing strategy. Metrics like reach, impressions, the share of voice, NPS, brand loyalty, and brand associations can help you learn how your target market feels about and values your brand. Use this data to improve your marketing initiatives and set your company apart from the competition.

CHAPTER 7

PAY-PER-CLICK (PPC) METRICS: Cost-Per-Click (CPC), Click-Through Rate (CTR), And Conversion Rate

Pay-per-click (PPC) advertising is a popular and effective way to drive traffic to your website and generate leads or sales.

To measure the success of your PPC campaigns, you need to understand the key metrics that are used to evaluate performance. In this chapter, we will explore the three main metrics of PPC advertising: cost-per-click (CPC), click-through rate (CTR), and conversion rate.

Cost-per-Click (CPC)

Cost-per-click (CPC) is the amount you pay each time a user clicks on your ad. This metric is important because it helps you understand the cost-effectiveness of your PPC campaigns. To calculate CPC, simply divide the total cost of your campaign by the number of clicks.

CPC can vary widely depending on factors such as the competitiveness of your industry, the targeting options you use, and the quality of your ad copy and landing page. To optimize your CPC, you can adjust your bids, refine your targeting, and improve your ad and landing page quality.

Click-through Rate (CTR)

Click-through rate (CTR) is the percentage of users who click on your ad after seeing it.

This metric is important because it helps you understand how effective your ad copy and targeting are in generating interest and engagement from your target audience.

To calculate CTR, simply divide the number of clicks by the number of impressions (or views).

A high CTR is generally a good indicator that your ads are resonating with your target audience and that you are reaching the right people with your targeting. To improve CTR, you can test different ad copy, adjust your targeting, and optimize your landing pages for a better user experience.

Conversion Rate

Conversion rate is the percentage of users who complete a desired action after clicking on your ad, such as making a purchase or filling out a form.

This metric is important because it helps you understand the ROI of your PPC campaigns and how effective your ad and landing page experience are in driving conversions.

To calculate the conversion rate, simply divide the number of conversions by the number of clicks.

A high conversion rate is generally a good indicator that your ad and landing page experience is well-targeted and compelling to your target audience.

To improve your conversion rate, you can test different ad and landing page variations, simplify the conversion process, and target more qualified traffic.

In conclusion, understanding the key metrics of PPC advertising - cost-per-click (CPC), click-through rate (CTR), and conversion rate - is essential for measuring the success of your campaigns and optimizing for better results.

By analyzing these metrics and making adjustments to your ad and targeting strategy, you can drive more traffic to your website, generate more leads or sales, and improve the ROI of your PPC campaigns.

CHAPTER 8

SEARCH ENGINE OPTIMIZATION (SEO) METRICS: Analyzing Organic Traffic, Keyword Rankings, and Backlinks

The following is a list of the most common questions we get from our customers.

To rank better in search engine results pages (SERPs) for pertinent keywords and phrases, you must optimize your website and content. You must comprehend the crucial performance indicators to gauge the success of your SEO efforts. The three primary SEO KPIs of organic traffic, keyword ranks, and backlinks will be examined in this chapter.

Natural Traffic

The number of visitors who find your website through unpaid search engine results is referred to as organic traffic. This indicator is crucial because it enables you to gauge how well your SEO campaigns are working to drive targeted traffic to your website.

You can make use of applications like Google Analytics to monitor organic traffic.

Several variables, like the level of industry competition, the value and applicability of your content, and the technical efficiency of your website, can have a significant impact on your website's organic traffic.

You can concentrate on producing high-quality content that satisfies user intent, optimizing your website for search engines, and advertising your material through social media and other channels to increase organic traffic.

Keyword Positioning

The position of your website and its pages in search engine results pages (SERPs) for pertinent keywords and phrases is referred to as keyword rankings.

This indicator is crucial because it reveals how effectively your website is prepared for particular search terms and how well your content matches user intent. You can use programs like SEMrush, Ahrefs, or Google Search Console to monitor keyword rankings.

The competitiveness of the phrase, the relevancy of your content, and the type and number of backlinks leading to your website are just a few examples of the variables that can greatly affect keyword rankings.

You can concentrate on optimizing your content and website for particular keywords, constructing quality backlinks, and monitoring and modifying your strategy in light of performance data to enhance keyword rankings.

Backlinks

Backlinks are links to your website that come from other websites. They are crucial to SEO because they let search engines know what other websites value and find your material relevant.

Moreover, backlinks can increase your site's traffic and your authority and trustworthiness in your sector. You can track backlinks using programs like Ahrefs or Majestic.

The amount and variety of connecting domains, the quality and relevancy of the linking website, the anchor text used in the connection, and other elements can all have a significant impact on backlinks.

You can concentrate on producing shareable and linkable high-quality content, contacting other websites for link possibilities, and monitoring and managing your backlink profile to prevent low-quality connections and penalties.

To sum up, it is crucial to comprehend the important SEO indicators of organic traffic, keyword ranks, and backlinks to evaluate your effort effort sande for more effective outcomes.

You may increase relevant traffic to your site, raise your rankings for particular keywords and phrases, and establish a powerful and reliable online presence in your sector by evaluating these indicators and modifying your content and SEO approach.

CHAPTER 9

CUSTOMER RELATIONSHIP MANAGEMENT (CRM) METRICS: Tracking Acquisition, Retention, and Lifetime Value (LTV)

Customer relationship management (CRM) is a strategy that businesses use to manage interactions with customers and improve customer satisfaction and loyalty.

To measure the success of your CRM efforts, you need to understand the key metrics that are used to evaluate performance.

In this chapter, we will explore the three main metrics of CRM: acquisition, retention, and lifetime value (LTV).

Acquisition

Acquisition refers to the process of acquiring new customers. This metric is important because it helps you understand how effective your marketing and sales efforts are in attracting and converting new customers. To track acquisition, you can use tools such as Google Analytics or your CRM software.

The acquisition can vary widely depending on factors such as the channels and tactics you use to reach new customers, the quality and relevance of your messaging, and the competitiveness of your industry. To improve acquisition, you can focus on creating targeted and effective marketing campaigns, optimizing your website and landing pages for conversions, and using customer data to personalize and optimize your outreach.

Retention

Retention refers to the ability to keep existing customers over time. This metric is important because it helps you understand how well your business is meeting the needs and expectations of your customers, and how likely they are to remain loyal and continue to purchase from you.

To track retention, you can use tools such as your CRM software or customer surveys and feedback.

Retention can vary widely depending on factors such as the quality and relevance of your products and services, the level of customer support and engagement you provide, and the competition and alternatives available in your industry.

To improve retention, you can focus on providing exceptional customer experiences, delivering ongoing value and benefits to your customers, and building strong relationships through personalized and proactive communication.

Lifetime Value (LTV)

Lifetime value (LTV) refers to the total value of a customer's purchases over the lifetime of their relationship with your business. This metric is important because it helps you understand the long-term revenue potential of your customer base and how much you can invest in acquisition and retention efforts. To track LTV, you can use tools such as your CRM software or customer data analysis.

LTV can vary widely depending on factors such as the frequency and volume of purchases, the average order value, and the customer's likelihood to refer and recommend your business to others.

To improve LTV, you can focus on providing exceptional customer experiences and value that incentivize repeat purchases and referrals, using targeted and personalized marketing to encourage upsells and cross-sells, and investing in loyalty and retention programs.

you can identify areas where you need to improve and focus your efforts on specific strategies that will yield the best results. It's important to note that these metrics are interconnected and dependent on each other, so it's essential to focus on all three to achieve long-term success.

The acquisition helps you attract and convert new customers, retention helps you keep existing customers and build loyalty, and LTV helps you understand the long-term value of your customer base.

By focusing on these metrics and continually optimizing your strategies, you can improve customer satisfaction and loyalty, drive revenue growth, and gain a competitive edge in your industry.

In addition to tracking and analyzing these metrics, it's also important to align your CRM strategies with your business goals and objectives.

This will help ensure that your efforts are focused on the most impactful areas and that you're making data-driven decisions that will yield the best results.

By combining a deep understanding of your customers with strategic analysis and optimization, you can create a powerful CRM strategy that drives growth and success for your business.

CHAPTER 10

DATA ANALYSIS TECHNIQUES: Using Analytics Tools and Methods to Gain Insights

Write me a thorough, knowledgeable, and interesting article about data analysis techniques. Gaining Insights using Analytics Tools and Techniques

Data analysis is essential for assessing the success of your marketing initiatives. You can track your performance metrics, track insights into customer behavior, and find areas for improvement with the use of analytics tools and approaches.

We'll look at a few of the modern marketers' best tools for data analysis in this chapter.

Google Analytics

You can measure and examine website traffic, user behavior, and conversions using this free analytics tool. With Google Analytics, you may create unique reports, monitor particular objectives and occurrences, and discover the success of your marketing initiatives.

With the use of the visualization method known as "heat mapping," you can examine how visitors engage with your website. You may learn which parts of your website are the most interesting and which are frustrating or confusing by monitoring clicks, scrolls, and other user behavior.

A/B testing compares two different iterations of a website or marketing campaign to determine which one performs better.

You may determine the most successful versions and make data-driven decisions about which components to include in future ads by testing various headlines, pictures, calls to action, and other components.

Sentiment analysis is a technique for examining internet content, including social media, to ascertain the general attitude of your customers. You may learn more about how your customers feel about your brand, goods, and services by looking at keywords and phrases.

Regression Analysis

A statistical method known as regression analysis allows you to examine the relationship between two or more variables. You may learn which elements have the most effects on your marketing performance by examining the correlation between various data.

Cohort Analysis

A technique for studying groups of customers based on shared traits is cohort analysis. You may spot trends and patterns in client retention, conversion rates, and other metrics by monitoring consumer behavior over time.

You may understand your clients and the success of your marketing activities better by utilizing these and other data analysis tools. You may promote growth, boost revenue, and acquire a competitive edge in your sector by using data-driven decisions and ongoing strategy optimization.

It's crucial to remember that data analysis methods are only as useful as the data you gather. You must make sure that your data is correct, pertinent, and current.

Setting up appropriate tracking and measurement systems as well as routinely evaluating and updating your data is required.

Furthermore, it's crucial to establish exactly what you hope to accomplish with your data analysis. Are you attempting to pinpoint problem areas, monitor consumer behavior, or assess the success of your marketing initiatives? You can make sure that you're employing the best data analysis approaches for your particular needs by clearly identifying your goals and objectives.

Finally, it's critical to have a competent staff of marketing experts and data analysts that can assist you in gathering, analyzing, and interpreting your data.

This staff should be well-versed in your company's aims and objectives, as well as technically proficient in the usage of analytics tools and techniques.

You may learn a lot about your clients and the efficacy of your marketing efforts by employing data analysis tools and procedures properly. You may use these insights to guide data-driven decisions that will help your organization develop and succeed.

CHAPTER 11

INTERPRETING DATA: Turning Metrics into Actionable Insights

Collecting and analyzing data is only the first step in measuring the impact of your marketing efforts. The real value comes from turning those metrics into actionable insights that can inform your marketing strategies and drive growth for your business.

In this chapter, we'll explore how to interpret data and turn metrics into actionable insights.

Identify Trends and Patterns

One of the first steps in interpreting data is to identify trends and patterns. By looking at metrics over time, you can identify trends and patterns that can inform your marketing strategies. For example, if you notice that certain products or services are consistently more popular than others, you may want to focus your marketing efforts on those areas.

Segment Your Data

Another important step in interpreting data is to segment your data by different variables such as demographics, geography, or behavior.

This can help you identify patterns and trends that are unique to specific customer segments, allowing you to tailor your marketing strategies to those groups.

Compare Metrics

Comparing metrics can also help you gain valuable insights. For example, comparing the conversion rates of different marketing channels can help you determine which channels are most effective at driving conversions.

This information can help you allocate your marketing budget more effectively.

Use Visualization Tools

Visualization tools such as charts, graphs, and heat maps can help you better understand your data and identify patterns and trends. By visualizing your data, you can quickly identify areas that require attention and take action accordingly.

Use Statistical Analysis

Statistical analysis can help you gain deeper insights into your data and identify correlations between different metrics. For example, you may find that certain customer behaviors are correlated with higher conversion rates. This information can help you tailor your marketing strategies to target those specific behaviors.

Combine Data Sources

Finally, it's important to combine data from different sources to gain a more complete understanding of your customers and their behavior. For example, combining data from your CRM system with data from your website analytics can help you gain insights into customer lifetime value and retention.

In addition to the steps outlined above, some additional techniques can help you interpret data and gain deeper insights into your marketing efforts. These include:

A/B Testing

A/B testing involves creating two versions of a marketing campaign or website and comparing the performance of each version.

By testing different variables such as headlines, calls to action, and images, you can identify what works best for your audience and optimize your campaigns accordingly.

Customer Surveys

Customer surveys can help you gather qualitative data about your customers' preferences, opinions, and behaviors. This information can be used to supplement your quantitative data and provide deeper insights into customer behavior.

Attribution Modeling

Attribution modeling involves assigning credit to different marketing channels for driving conversions. By understanding which channels are most effective at driving conversions, you can optimize your marketing budget and allocate resources more effectively.

Cohort Analysis

Cohort analysis involves grouping customers by a shared characteristic such as the date they signed up or the product they purchased. By analyzing customer behavior within these cohorts, you can gain insights into how customer behavior changes over time and tailor your marketing strategies accordingly.

Predictive Analytics

Predictive analytics involves using data, statistical algorithms, and machine learning techniques to identify future trends and behaviors. By predicting customer behavior, you can proactively optimize your marketing strategies and stay ahead of the competition

By interpreting data effectively, you can turn metrics into actionable insights that inform your marketing strategies and drive growth for your business. By regularly reviewing and analyzing your data, you can identify areas for improvement, optimize your marketing campaigns, and stay ahead of the competition.

CHAPTER 12

OPTIMIZATION STRATEGIES: Leveraging Insights to Optimize Marketing Campaigns

The next stage is to use the data you've gathered and analyzed about your marketing efforts to improve your campaigns.

Using data-driven insights, optimization strategies let you decide how to deploy resources and modify your marketing plans. Here are some crucial optimization tactics to take into account:

Targeting

Determine the characteristics and habits of your most valuable consumers using customer data. Use this data to more precisely target your marketing campaigns, adjusting your language and offerings to better suit the requirements and preferences of your target market.

Budget Allocation

Determine which marketing initiatives and channels are most successful in generating sales using data. Give these channels and campaigns more of your marketing budget, and change or drop the ones that aren't working as well.

Messaging and Creative

Employ A/B testing to compare various messages, creative pieces, and calls to action to see which ones your target audience responds to the most favorably. Use these data to improve consumer engagement and conversion with your messaging and creativity.

Use data to determine the best times of day for your clients to interact with your marketing messaging. To increase engagement and conversions, adjust the timing of your advertising accordingly.

Personalization

Tailor your marketing offerings and communications using information about your customers. You can increase engagement and conversions by adjusting your messaging and offers to the unique requirements and preferences of your customers.

Testing and Optimization

To continually enhance your marketing strategies, use constant testing and optimization. Use data to pinpoint areas that need development, and test out alternative approaches to discover which ones are most effective with your audience.

You can enhance the impact of your marketing efforts and improve results for your company by using data to guide your marketing decisions and consistently optimizing your campaigns. Remember to stay nimble and attentive to changes in customer behavior and market trends, and be willing to adapt your plans as needed to stay ahead of the competition.

CHAPTER 13

CASE STUDIES: Real-World Examples of Effective Marketing Measurement and Analysis

A potent tool for demonstrating the importance of efficient marketing measurement and analysis is the case study.

You can obtain knowledge and inspiration for your own company by studying actual cases of businesses that have successfully used data to enhance their marketing initiatives.

Here are some instances of measuring and analysis in marketing that work well:

Amazon

Amazon is renowned for its highly developed data analytics skills, which enable the business to tailor marketing offers and communications to specific customers.

Amazon can recommend goods and deals that are very relevant and interesting to each client by gathering information on their behavior and preferences.

HubSpot

HubSpot is a marketing automation platform that focuses on inbound marketing as the foundation of its operations.

HubSpot has had amazing development and success as a result of its ability to continuously fine-tune and upgrade its marketing strategies through the use of data to monitor and assess the efficacy of its inbound marketing initiatives.

Airbnb

Airbnb has significantly improved its client acquisition and retention efforts through the use of data.

The most effective marketing channels and strategies for generating conversions have been identified by Airbnb through analysis of consumer behavior and preference data, and the company has tailored its marketing campaigns appropriately.

Coca-Cola

Coca-Cola has developed incredibly successful marketing strategies that connect with consumers by utilizing data. Coca-Cola has developed customized marketing messages and campaigns that connect with customers emotionally and increase brand loyalty and sales by gathering data on consumer behavior and preferences.

Dollar Shave Club is a subscription-based company that offers the sale of razors and other personal care items.

Dollar Shave Club has achieved excellent growth and client retention rates by using customer data analysis to develop highly personalized marketing messages and offers that connect with specific customers.

The effectiveness of accurate marketing measurement and analysis is demonstrated by these case studies. These businesses have developed highly targeted and successful marketing efforts that promote growth and success by gathering and evaluating data on customer behavior, preferences, and campaign efficacy.

You can improve your outcomes and accomplish your business objectives by applying a data-driven strategy to your marketing initiatives.

CHAPTER 14

CHALLENGES AND SOLUTIONS: Overcoming Common Obstacles in Measuring Marketing Impact

Measuring the impact of your marketing efforts is crucial for achieving your business goals and staying competitive in today's fast-paced digital landscape.

However, several challenges can make it difficult to effectively measure the impact of your marketing campaigns. Here are some common obstacles to measuring marketing impact, as well as solutions for overcoming them:

Lack of Data

One of the biggest challenges in measuring marketing impact is a lack of data. Without sufficient data, it can be difficult to identify trends, track progress, and make informed decisions about your marketing efforts.

To overcome this challenge, it's important to establish clear data collection processes and invest in tools and technologies that can help you gather and analyze data more effectively.

Inaccurate Data

Another challenge in measuring marketing impact is inaccurate data. If your data is incomplete or contains errors, it can lead to incorrect conclusions and ineffective decision-making. To overcome this challenge, it's important to establish data validation processes and invest in technologies that can help you identify and correct inaccuracies in your data.

Lack of Alignment

Measuring marketing impact requires collaboration and alignment between marketing teams and other departments, such as sales, finance, and IT.

However, it can be challenging to align teams with different goals and priorities. To overcome this challenge, it's important to establish clear goals and metrics that are aligned across all departments and to foster a culture of collaboration and communication.

Difficulty in Attribution

Attribution is the process of assigning credit to different marketing channels and tactics for driving specific actions, such as conversions or sales.

However, it can be difficult to accurately attribute actions to specific marketing efforts, especially in complex customer journeys.

To overcome this challenge, it's important to establish clear attribution models and invest in technologies that can help you track and analyze customer behavior across different touchpoints.

Limited Resources

Measuring marketing impact requires significant resources, including time, money, and expertise. However, many companies have limited resources and may struggle to invest in measurement and analysis.

To overcome this challenge, it's important to prioritize measurement and analysis as a key part of your marketing strategy and to leverage cost-effective tools and technologies that can help you gather and analyze data more efficiently.

By addressing these common obstacles to measuring marketing impact, you can overcome the challenges and gain the insights you need to make informed decisions and drive growth for your business.

With the right strategies and tools in place, you can effectively measure the impact of your marketing campaigns and optimize your efforts for success.

CHAPTER 15

CONCLUSION: The Future of Marketing Measurement and Analytics

Because of technological improvements and the rising significance of data-driven decision-making, marketing measurement, and analytics have advanced significantly in recent years.

Efficient monitoring and analysis are essential for success and staying ahead of the competition as firms continue to fight in a fast-paced digital market.

Yet, marketing analytics and measurement are always changing. The following are some major developments and forecasts for marketing measurement and analytics going forward:

More Focus on Customer Experience: In the upcoming years, assessing and improving the customer experience will probably receive more attention.

This calls for a more comprehensive measurement strategy that takes the full client journey into account rather than simply certain touchpoints.

It's a good idea to have a backup plan in case the backup fails. Marketers will be able to get more in-depth information and decide on their campaigns with greater knowledge as a result.

Concentrate on Real-Time Insights

Real-time analytics will play a bigger role in marketing measurement in the future since they let companies immediately spot trends and opportunities and take swift action in response to shifting market conditions.

More Customized and Relevant Marketing: Companies will be able to deliver more Personalized and Relevant Marketing campaigns as they continue to collect more data about their clients.

To do this, a stronger emphasis will need to be placed on data analysis and customer segmentation as well as a deeper comprehension of client demands and preferences.

Increased Marketing and Sales Integration: It will be crucial to combine marketing and sales data and analytics to fully comprehend the effects of marketing initiatives.

Businesses will be able to better track customer journeys and link activities to certain marketing campaigns thanks to this.

The growing significance of data privacy and security is another development that will influence how marketing measurement and analytics are conducted in the future.

As consumers grow more aware of the value of their data, businesses will need to be more honest about how they gather, use, and preserve data. Businesses will also need to be proactive in preventing data breaches and cyberattacks that compromise client information.

The integration of physical and online data is a crucial area of attention for the future of marketing measurement and analytics. Businesses must be able to track client interactions across all channels and touchpoints, both online and offline, as omnichannel marketing becomes more prevalent.

As a result, data management and integration will need to be given more attention, as well as a more complicated and sophisticated approach to data analysis.

Improvements in data reporting and visualization will also influence the direction of marketing measurement and analytics. Businesses will need to collect more data, and it will be crucial to present that data in a way that enables decision-makers to spot trends and insights right away.

This calls for a stronger emphasis on data storytelling and visualization, as well as a more approachable method of data reporting.

In conclusion, the future of marketing analytics and measurement is both promising and difficult. Businesses may optimize their marketing strategies, learn more about client behavior, and ultimately help their businesses grow and succeed by keeping up with the most recent trends and technologies.

Nevertheless, to do so calls for a dedication to lifelong learning and growth, as well as a readiness to change and grow in response to shifting market circumstances and client demands.

Businesses may use the power of marketing measurement and analytics to achieve their objectives and succeed in today's cutthroat industry by putting the correct strategies and tools in place.